AF270610

History's Greatest Mysteries

DiscoverRoo
An Imprint of Pop!
popbooksonline.com

HISTORY'S
ODDEST
EVENTS

by Grace Hansen

abdobooks.com

Published by Pop!, a division of ABDO, PO Box 398166, Minneapolis, Minnesota 55439. Copyright © 2023 by Abdo Consulting Group, Inc. International copyrights reserved in all countries. No part of this book may be reproduced in any form without written permission from the publisher. DiscoverRoo™ is a trademark and logo of Pop!.

Printed in the United States of America, North Mankato, Minnesota.

052022
092022

THIS BOOK CONTAINS RECYCLED MATERIALS

Cover Photos: Shutterstock Images

Interior Photos: Shutterstock Images; Getty Images; AP Image Collection; Alamy

Editor: Elizabeth Andrews
Series Designer: Candice Keimig

Library of Congress Control Number: 2021951845

Publisher's Cataloging-in-Publication Data

Names: Hansen, Grace, author.

Title: History's oddest events / by Grace Hansen

Description: Minneapolis, Minnesota : Pop, 2023 | Series: History's greatest mysteries | Includes online resources and index

Identifiers: ISBN 9781098242299 (lib. bdg.) | 9781098242992 (ebook)

Subjects: LCSH: Oddities--Juvenile literature. | Curiosities and wonders--Juvenile literature.

Classification: DDC 509--dc23

WELCOME TO DiscoverRoo!

Pop open this book and you'll find QR codes loaded with information, so you can learn even more!

Scan this code* and others like it while you read, or visit the website below to make this book pop!

popbooksonline.com/oddest-events

*Scanning QR codes requires a web-enabled smart device with a QR code reader app and a camera.

TABLE OF CONTENTS

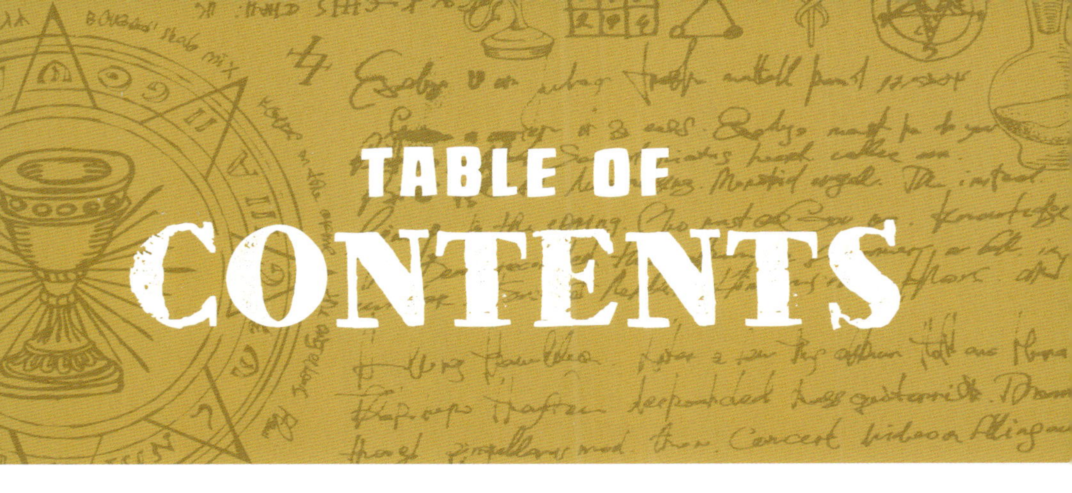

AN EVENT FOR THE AGES

Think about all the things that can happen in one year. Now think about all that can happen in thousands and thousands of years! Since the beginning of the human age, people have learned, changed, explored, battled, lost, and prevailed. All these things and more have

led to events that we can read about in

history books. And some of those events

happen to be a little odder than others.

Celebrating birthdays and anniversaries makes for happy and memorable events.

CHAPTER 2

THE LOST COLONY

In 1587, Sir Walter Raleigh and Queen Elizabeth I of England sent more than 100 people to America to start a **colony**. Others had gone before but returned when it proved too difficult. But life in England was not much better. The country was overcrowded and at war with Spain. Having colonies in America would help England in many ways.

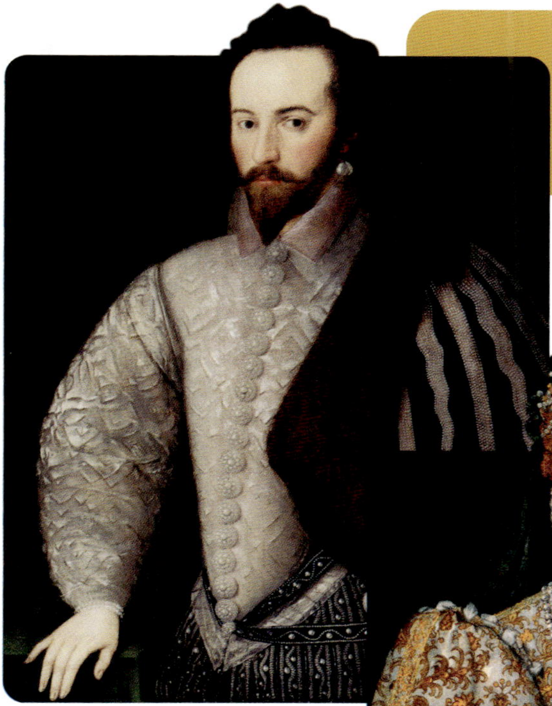

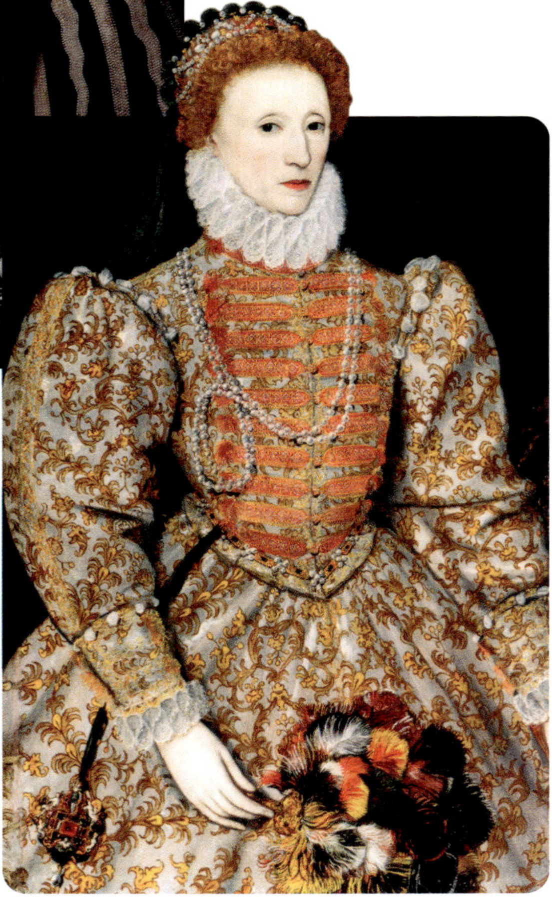

Queen Elizabeth I *(bottom) and her advisor, Sir Walter Raleigh (top), agreed that having colonies in America would help England in the war against Spain.*

As the ship approached the continent, the captain stopped at Roanoke Island. He demanded they build there instead of the agreed upon location farther north in Chesapeake Bay. The new colonists exited the ship. Among them was John White, an artist. Raleigh had chosen him to govern the new colony. White's pregnant daughter, Eleanor Dare, was there too.

The colonists got to work right away. But as the weeks went by, life in the new colony was not getting easier. The group was already very low on food and other

supplies. So, they sent White back to

England to gather more.

Eleanor Dare gave birth to daughter Virginia Dare on August 18, 1587. Virginia was the first English person born on American soil.

Due to the war, White could not return

to America until 1590. He was excited

to see his granddaughter, Virginia, who

was now three years old. But there was

not a soul to be found on Roanoke.

White came upon a tree that had *CRO*

carved into it, and then a post that read

CROATOAN. Croatoan was the name

of an **indigenous** tribe and an island

50 miles (80.5km) away. There was no

cross etched above the words, meaning

the colonists felt safe. White and the

crew planned to go to Croatoan the

next morning. But bad weather and low

supplies made it impossible. White was

forced to leave and never returned.

Since 1590, there have been many theories about what happened to the Roanoke colonists. Some historians believe the colonists starved, died of

John White drew the neighboring indigenous tribes' ways of life.

disease, or were killed. Others are more
optimistic. The colonists may have been
invited to join Indigenous tribes. There are
stories about English-speaking people
living with local tribes. There were also
accounts of tribe members with blue
eyes and blonde hair, features that would
be very unusual for an indigenous person
at the time.

SIGNIFICANT LOCATIONS

The map shows some significant locations for the Roanoke colonists and England. On one expedition to America, the English named Virginia in honor of Queen Elizabeth I. North Carolina was named later to honor King Charles I of England.

Still, after hundreds of years, no one

knows for certain what happened to the

Roanoke colonists, and maybe never will.

Houses in Colonial America often had just one room. They had dirt floors and a fireplace. Most had open windows, as glass was very expensive.

CHAPTER 3

BATTLE OF THE BUNNIES

Napoleon Bonaparte was a French military and political leader. And in 1807 he was one of the most powerful men in the world. In July of that year, Napoleon signed the Treaties of Tilsit. One of these **treaties** ended the war between France and Imperial Russia. To **commemorate**

the occasion, Napoleon planned a rabbit hunt. Louis-Alexandre Berthier, Napoleon's chief of staff, gathered around 3,000 rabbits from nearby farms. Napoleon gathered his top military officers.

Jacques-Louis David's Napoleon Crossing the Alps *is perhaps the most famous painting of the military leader.*

Everyone was impressed by the

number of rabbits Berthier managed to

collect. The men were excited to hunt!

They readied their

guns, and the signal

was given to

open the cages.

Trumpets sounded

and the rabbits

bolted from their

Napoleon surely did not want the people of France or his foes to find out about the rabbit hunt.

confined quarters. But instead of running away from the hunters, thousands of very hungry bunnies ran toward them!

Berthier didn't know that **domestic**

bunnies related humans to food. And

the bunnies had not eaten for at least a

whole day. Before the men knew what to do, they were **engulfed** in rabbits. The fluffy militia swarmed Napoleon and climbed his legs. He kicked and yelled and wrestled the bunnies off himself. He ran to his carriage, but he wasn't safe there either. Napoleon, the military genius, was forced to retreat.

CHAPTER 4

DANCE TO THE DEATH

In July 1518, a woman known as Frau Troffea stood in the streets of Strasbourg in Europe. Suddenly, she began to shake, sway, and spin. The other villagers looked at her confused and wondered what she was doing. She was dancing and she didn't stop. Soon others joined her.

Onlookers could not understand why some of their neighbors would not stop dancing.

A concerned council of citizens went to local doctors for advice. The doctors believed the dancers were suffering from overheated blood. But what was the

cure? The doctors said to let them dance!

The council had a stage built and even

hired musicians.

The dancing plague did not just strike Strasbourg. It was common throughout mainland Europe between the 14th and 17th centuries.

Over the next few months, upwards of 400 people danced without end. But the doctors' "cure" did not seem to help. The dancers' bodies were exhausted. They collapsed after twirling under the summer sun for hours. As many as 15 people a day may have died. The council decided they were dealing with a curse. They stopped the music and brought the

St. Vitus is the patron saint of dancers. It was believed in Strasbourg that if the saint was not pleased with you, you'd be cursed to dance.

disturbed dancers to a shrine for Saint Vitus. After a few weeks, the movements finally ceased.

Historians have wondered what caused the dancing. For some time, it was believed that food poisoning was the culprit. There is a **fungus** that can

grow on grains. When consumed it can cause **hallucinations**. But the more commonly agreed upon theory is **mass hysteria** brought on by extreme stress.

STRESS IN STRASBOURG

Strasbourg and its surrounding areas had been dealing with hunger and disease in the years leading up to the dancing plague. It was a very difficult time to say the least. The locals believed that St. Vitus was unhappy with them. Some may have started to dance to please the saint, leading to a mass-hysteria event.

MAKING CONNECTIONS

TEXT-TO-SELF

What is the oddest event you've ever heard about? How was it similar to the events in this book?

TEXT-TO-TEXT

Have you read any other books about interesting events in history? What did those books have in common with this one?

TEXT-TO-WORLD

Do you think that great amounts of stress can cause people to do things they would not normally do? Explain your answer.

GLOSSARY

assassinated — murdered for political reasons.

colony — a place where a group of people come to live which is under the control of their home country.

commemorate — to celebrate an event, person, or situation by doing something special.

domestic — living with humans instead of in the wild.

engulfed — covered entirely, as if by a flood.

fungus — one of a large group of living things that appear similar to plants. Fungi consume plant, animal, and other living matter.

hallucination — a false or distorted but convincing sensory perception.

indigenous — the earliest known inhabitants of a place.

mass hysteria — a large group of people experiencing an uncontrollable outburst of fear or other emotions, producing fits of irrational behavior.

treaty — a formal agreement between two or more countries.

INDEX

ONLINE RESOURCES
popbooksonline.com

Scan this code* and others

like it while you read, or visit

the website below to make

this book pop!

popbooksonline.com/oddest-events

*Scanning QR codes requires a web-enabled smart device with a QR code reader app and a camera.